The ABC's of Psychic Development

Awareness, Belief & Courage

By Laura Lyn

Blessings & Light,
Laura Lyn

Also by Laura Lyn

Finding Your Inner Mystic - The Art of Self Discovery Oracle Cards

Healing With the Angel Rays - Simply Ask and Believe

(All titles are available online at: angelreader.net)

Contents

Acknowledgements

My greatest appreciation for the development and work that has gone into this project goes to Dale Lute. This model would have never been realized without Dale's awareness and sustained belief that everybody should have the opportunity to learn and grow spiritually through psychic senses and meditation. Dale's words can be read throughout this workbook. Thanks so much for your heart and love. My heartfelt thanks also goes to Jessica Fisher for her time and talents in editing, proofreading and cover design. You are a gift and I am most grateful. Thank you Russell and Deborah Lute for proofreading, and your channeled messages that spirit inspired you to bring forward. I would like to thank Louis Charles for his contribution to the Spirit Rescue chapter. To the Angel Rays, you have been a wonderful inspiration. Keep shining on for there is so much light and Spirit to share!

Introduction

The premise of this workbook is to teach what I have learned over the years about psychic abilities and how to use them. Before we get into this workbook please allow me to share some fundamental truths that I have learned on the subject.

I believe the psychic senses that are in our body are actually determined by a well orchestrated plan using a multitude of muscles, organs and extended energies. Psychic abilities, like all abilities, take practice and repetition to achieve good results. Here are methods I use to keep practicing and exercising my psychic muscle.

- Listen to tranquil music.
- Burn candles and pay attention to their flame when questing.
- I always, every day without exception pray first thing when I wake up. I pray for opportunities to help and to share the love.
- When going to bed at night I always say thank you to Spirit for the gifts received and gifts that I could bring to others in love.

The essence of love comes from within and it can be a welcome acquired energy when you are working with light sources. Everything that I will teach comes from this place of love. This workbook will focus on spiritual guidance through angels, enlightened beings, and loved ones who have captured light within.

Love is always the answer. When being psychically attacked, love is the best defense. The work you will learn comes from the heart. When bringing true compassion and your heart energy forward to understand and help someone in need (alive or those who have passed on), you are bringing love. In that space the highest psychic world will open up and you will have a plethora of opportunities to see, hear, feel, and to know the existence of energy.

The A,B,C's - Awareness, Belief and Courage are the basis of this book. Awareness is essential - Being aware that you are never alone, spirit is always around. Believing is absolutely necessary in order to feel and see the energy. Courage is extremely important in this work. Fear has no place in the psychic world.

There are many exercises within this book that have enough space to allow you to write down your experiences. I encourage you to write as much as possible in the space provided.

Introduction

This book will be your own personal journal that will help you track your progress as you develop. You will be pleasantly surprised at how your thoughts advance and change over the course of this workbook and for years to come.

Enjoy the learning process and know that you are never alone, for there are wonderful high energy light sources right by your side!

Love and blessings,
Laura Lyn

Chapter One

∞

Feel the Energy

Attuning to the White Light

Practice every morning imagining that you are encompassed with a beautiful white light. Imagine the white light enveloping you and forming a protective circle around your body. Become familiar with this white light until you make it your own. Over time you will learn to work with this light for protection, healing, and awareness.

Attuning the Chakras

Imagine the colors of the chakras in relation to your body. Starting with violet for the crown chakra, moving to indigo for the third eye, then blue for the throat, and green for the heart, yellow for the solar plexus, orange for sacral and red for the base chakra. Become attuned and familiar with these colors and from there you can learn to balance them. *If you are not familiar with the chakras and their meanings, there is more detail in the reference section at the end of this book.*

Build a Psychic Shield

When one starts to use and work with their psychic energy, it becomes necessary to build a personal psychic shield. We don't want our energy to be drained by others or any negative influences to penetrate our psychic energy. Imagine a shield of radiant white light surrounding your body. Ask this shield of white light to protect you from any negative or intruding energy. Ask that only positive, uplifting energy be allowed through.

Remember the ABC's

Awareness - Awareness of who you are. You are spirit and spirit is all around you. Be in tune with every characteristic of you. Reflect on how you and all are connected. This realization brings a deeper love and respect for everything that will make the unconstructive aspects in life insignificant. Allow your body to become a barometer of truth.

Belief - Trusting the information that your intuition is giving you is essential for your overall development. Many times, students say they sensed things all the time, but regarded what they were feeling was "just my imagination". After learning this material, many of them have learned to bring their gifts forward and help those in need.

Courage - The leap of faith that you take when tapping into your psychic self is a monumental challenge. Have the courage to ask, feel, discern, and speak. Releasing fear is essential for growth and internal awareness. Believing in your self is key to conquering fear. This is where courage begins.

Write your thoughts about the ABC's

_____

_____

_____

_____

_____

_____

_____

_____

_____

How Do You Feel Energy?

We all have a certain capacity to sense energy. Many people may never be aware of what they are sensing, even though every aspect of their lives is influenced by the energies around them.

Watch a young child and you will discover that they can sense more than an average adult. Many children naturally communicate with "imaginary friends." As a child grows up, he or she is distracted by the material world. The influence of society and belief structures may also weaken a child's senses. Most people lose touch with this natural ability that they were born with while they are still very young.

The information presented here is intended to get you reacquainted with your abilities. You will find that every exercise presented will help you on your path to reconnect with your true self.

Psychic Abilities and What They Mean

There are many types of psychic abilities. Most people have felt one or more of the abilities described here. Read over each type of psychic gift to see which abilities you have experienced.

- **The Aura** is the energy that originates from living beings. People with the ability to see auras can know much about a person by seeing their colors.
- **Channeling** is the ability to receive communication from spirit. Angels, guides, and loved ones can communicate through someone who is tuned in to this ability.
- **Clairalience** is the psychic ability to sense smell. People who have clairalience will sometimes smell aromas and odors that come from the spirit world. Examples are cigarette smoke, perfume, baking bread.....
- **Clairaudience** is the psychic power of 'hearing'. People who have tuned in to this can hear voices from other realms and times. Hearing voices can be with your ears or within your mind.
- **Clairkenesis** is the term given for the ability to feel the angels, guides, and loved ones whom have passed.
- **Clairsentience** means the ability to sense subtle feelings or emotions. A person who is tuned in to this ability may have a knowing of unseen details that others may not perceive.
- **Clairvoyance** means the ability to see or visualize. This ability to "see" can be with your eyes or through your mind's eye. Clairvoyants may see angels, ghosts, spirits, or guides.
- **Empathy** means the ability to feel emotions in many ways. An empath can feel mental and physical energies emitted by others. Personal emotions can be chaotic if the empath is not aware of, or has no control of their ability.

- **Intuition** is the apparent ability to acquire knowledge and answers without using details, logic or the use of reason, which is seemingly independent of any previous experience or observed understanding.
- **Mediumship** is the ability to communicate with other realms. A medium can communicate with angels, guides, and loved ones in a two way "conversation".
- **Precognition** is the capability to know events in the future, before they actually happen.
- **Psychometry** is the ability to know details about a person by touching the object he or she has touched.
- **Retro-cognition** refers to people who are able to see, hear and feel details about past lives.
- **Telepathy** is the ability to know what others are thinking.

The ABC's of Psychic Development

Exercise One - What Are Your Gifts?

In this exercise you will identify and evaluate the gifts that you have experienced. Read each of the "senses" listed below. Have you had a psychic experience with any of these?

Place a checkmark next to each one:

- ☐ See
- ☐ Hear
- ☐ Smell
- ☐ Feel or just "know"
- ☐ Sense emotions
- ☐ "Knowing" without details
- ☐ Receive messages
- ☐ Predict future events
- ☐ Know what others are thinking
- ☐ Converse with other realms
- ☐ Get details by touching objects
- ☐ See Auras

For each checked item, please answer the following questions.

1. Describe the details regarding each of the psychic gifts that you have experienced. *Can you think of anything that may have caused the ability? How often does it occur?*

_____

_____

_____

_____

_____

_____

_____

_____

2. Try to recall what happened and how you felt about your experience.
   Did it help you or someone else? Were you happy about the outcome?

_____

_____

_____

_____

_____

_____

_____

_____

_____

_____

_____

_____

_____

_____

_____

_____

_____

_____

3. Think about any information that you received.
   Was your experience validated afterwards?

_____

_____

_____

_____

_____

_____

_____

_____

_____

_____

_____

_____

_____

_____

_____

_____

Exercise Two – Connect With Yourself

Advancing your abilities may be difficult in our busy, distracting environment. You may feel helpless or even overwhelmed in today's society. There appears to be so much turmoil and chaos throughout the world. How can you turn this around?

Connecting with yourself through love, respect, and absolute honesty can give great insights on your purpose in life. This is something that must come from within and may take a great effort to accomplish. Once you're in that place of love for yourself, you will find that the effort was well worth it.

When you love yourself, the world will love you back!

List how you can accomplish each item listed below.

    1. Be kind to yourself.

2. Be honest.

_____

_____

_____

_____

_____

_____

_____

_____

_____

3. Trust what you feel.

_____

_____

_____

_____

_____

_____

_____

_____

4. Show gratitude.

_____

_____

_____

_____

_____

_____

_____

_____

5. Release the past.

_____

_____

_____

_____

_____

_____

_____

_____

6. Find the good in situations.

_____

_____

_____

_____

_____

_____

_____

_____

_____

7. Live in the moment.

_____

_____

_____

_____

_____

_____

_____

_____

_____

Exercise Three - Self Discovery

Find which items below have meaning to you. Write what you feel you have done or what can be done to accomplish them.

1. Clarify who you are, your spiritual self.

_____

_____

_____

_____

_____

_____

_____

2. How can you set and hold conscious intentions?

_____

_____

_____

_____

_____

_____

_____

_____

3. What can you do to spark your creativity?

_____

_____

_____

_____

_____

_____

_____

_____

_____

4. List how effectively you use your imagination and stretch your mental abilities.

_____

_____

_____

_____

_____

_____

_____

_____

5. Release your buried inspiration. What are your dreams?

_____

_____

_____

_____

_____

_____

_____

_____

6. Explore your life purpose. List the most important here.

_____

_____

_____

_____

_____

_____

_____

_____

Be Still and Listen
Meditation is the Key to Awakening

Spirit communication is very subtle and takes dedication and focus to allow the messages to flow. Learning to relax the conscious mind is essential and often is the most difficult part of hearing the messages. By learning to still your thoughts and to be at a place of inner peace, you are allowing your internal conditions to be primed for hearing messages on all levels.

New patterns of thought are difficult to achieve, they take dedication and practice. Develop a plan and stick with it while not expecting immediate gratification. In time, the patience, practice, and dedication will pay off.

You are working towards calming your inner thoughts during meditation. It's not only about silencing, it's also about reacting properly when a thought comes in. Gently acknowledge the thought, and give yourself the gift of allowing the thought to gently drift away.

Meditation is an essential step in your personal development. I teach daily about the A,B,C's (Awareness, Belief, and Courage). The most critical point is courage. It takes a lot of work to become aware of and to open our senses in a profound way.

Outside stimulus can be distracting if we allow it to be. By practicing internal silence you are giving yourself the gift of space. Creating space within your mind will allow you to be open and ready for spirit messages.

Laura Lyn's Hints on Relaxing the Mind

1) No need to struggle. Allow the thoughts to float on by. By latching onto thoughts you actually sabotage yourself from the peaceful mindful gift you are trying to achieve. Remember it's all good, float on by. Give yourself keywords such as harmony and peace when a distracting thought comes up. Before long the thoughts will be nothing more than random words that have no meaning.

2) Don't give up. Give yourself fifteen minute sessions a couple times a day to start. Don't over practice for that will cause mind fatigue.

3) Be media free. Turn off all forms of distractions. Cell phones, TV, even the computer will make random noises. This will also eliminate electromagnetic field disturbances.

4) Same time, same place. Allow yourself to become a habitual meditator. By aligning yourself with daily practices of meditation structure and a five to thirty minute routine, you will quickly find yourself enjoying the bliss of mindful peace.

5) Repeat these words; awareness expands consciousness, awareness expands consciousness, awareness expands consciousness... By repeating these words you are allowing yourself to be extremely aware that you are part of it ALL and interconnected to everything and everyone.

6) You may find it useful to start with a guided meditation CD such as, *Finding Your Inner Mystic*, which is part of the next exercise.

Exercise Four – Guided Meditation

A guided meditation is great for beginners and experienced meditators. I recommend my *Finding Your Inner Mystic* CD for this exercise. You may use any guided meditation that you feel led to. Before you begin, use what you have learned in the previous section to prepare for this meditation. When you are done, write down what you saw and felt in the space provided.

_____

_____

_____

_____

_____

_____

_____

_____

_____

_____

_____

_____

_____

_____

_____

_____

_____

_____

_____

_____

Grounding – Focus, Love and Balance

Grounding yourself after doing energy work is important. If you find your thoughts drifting or have difficulty with focus, it's time to do some grounding. It's a good idea to make grounding a part of your daily routine. If you fail to ground properly, you will find yourself developing unhealthy habits because your body will attempt to automatically ground for you.

Grounding is simply getting back in touch with yourself and your surroundings. When you tap into your psychic abilities, you are tapping into subtle energies. Because we are spirit, our physical body is often neglected during this process.

The test below will point out the difficulties you may encounter if you're not properly grounded. Read over the questions and note which symptoms apply to you.

Grounding Test

- ☐ Do you get lost easily getting from point A to point B?
- ☐ Is it difficult for you to pay attention in the classroom?
- ☐ Have you noticed yourself feeling spacey?
- ☐ Does it take you longer than it should to do a simple task?
- ☐ Do you spend a lot of time dwelling on past situations?
- ☐ Do you avoid putting yourself in situations that require your full attention?
- ☐ Is it difficult for you to concentrate?
- ☐ Are you prone to accidents?
- ☐ Do you have difficulty staying on topic during group conversations?
- ☐ Do you feel that you are more often out of body than in body?
- ☐ Are you easily distracted?
- ☐ Do your emotions often get the better of you?

Grounding methods

Below is a list of healthy methods for grounding.

- Get back to nature. Explore the outdoors.
- Gardening is a great way to ground.
- Take a walk with no shoes.
- Native American Drumming.
- Take five minutes to appreciate the moment.

Grounding Meditation

This meditation can be done when you feel out of synch. Five to fifteen minutes should be plenty of time to get you back on track. If you are able, go outdoors and do this meditation in your bare feet. If that's not possible any location will do.

The next time you're feeling angry, stressed, confused etc., try the meditation below. After you've finished this short meditation, use the space below to write down your experience.

- Close your eyes, take a nice deep breath.
- Visualize yourself as a tree.
- Imagine roots growing out from your feet.
- Allow the roots to grow into the ground.
- As the roots grow, visualize the connections they make beneath the earth.
- Allow these connections to grow and interconnect throughout the planet.

What did you experience during the grounding meditation?

_____

_____

_____

_____

_____

_____

_____

_____

_____

_____

_____

_____

_____

_____

_____

_____

_____

_____

_____

_____

Crystals for Grounding

Crystal	Purpose
Hematite	Grounding and Shielding
Green Moss Agate	Balance and Strength
Bloodstone	Devotion and Wisdom
Smoky Quartz	Grounding and Manifestation
Red Jasper	Protection and Grounding

For more information on crystals, please read Crystals to Amplify the Energy in the reference section at the end of this workbook.

Homework – Letter to Spirit

Write a letter to your Angels, Spirit Guide or a loved one. In the body of the letter, simply ask the questions that you would like to know. Below is an example of a letter you may want to write.

Dear Angel (or Dear Guide),

Please share with me your name and what you look like. Please share your insights with me. When have you impacted my life? Have I seen you before?

Sincere love, thanks and appreciation _____

Make this letter a personal request to create a special connection. The purpose of the letter is to open up communication. After writing the letter, read it out loud and place it under your pillow. Reread the letter nightly asking that the guidance or loved one comes through during your dreams. Have a journal prepared for your dream work. Use the following section for any notes on this exercise. Within a week you should have some new insight about your spirit friend(s).

One more note: Always ask for protection before going to sleep. You are in a place of opening right now; at this point you can be vulnerable for lower energy disturbances. Always shield yourself; this will enable you to sleep more soundly during this shift.

Enjoy the messages!

Write down what you found out after writing your letter.

_____

_____

_____

_____

_____

_____

_____

_____

_____

_____

_____

_____

_____

_____

_____

_____

_____

_____

_____

_____

_____

_____

_____

About the Next Chapter......

The next chapter is titled *Mediumship*. We will cover spirit communication, divination, and protection.

Chapter One – Feel the Energy

Chapter Two

∞

Mediumship – Channeling

Spirit communicates with us daily in varied ways. I receive most of my spirit communication through translating symbols. For example, when I see a hawk gently gliding in the sky, I watch and listen. My internal point (Higher Self) hears the message. When I receive the message, I always say thank you. There are so many ways to receive communication from spirit.

I look through and at the world with eyes of listening. My eyes hear and my ears see. By calming your thoughts regarding immediate situations and looking outside the box, your world will open up in ways that are profound and highly empowering.

Spirit communication is so subtle that it can be missed. Daily, one hears songs but the words go unnoticed. A familiar person may walk by, but most do not take the time to consider who that person may be. A random thought goes by and is hardly acknowledged. By being focused, you are aligning to your Spirit Guides and the messages that are given daily.

Dreams are one means that spirit uses to communicate with us. Your higher self receives messages and works out solutions that aid in your development. Always have a journal or tablet available and take quick notes when you wake up. Your waking thoughts can be fleeting. Writing in your journal as you wake up is essential to remembering the messages you receive. You will be surprised at how much information filters in upon awakening.

This will go into a little bit of my philosophical beliefs regarding mediumship and channeling. First, it is important to differentiate between mediumship and channeling. Simply put, mediumship is the act of receiving messages from loved ones; channeling is receiving messages from spirit guides, angels, ascended masters and other enlightened beings. There can be confusion with this subject because the words used are often interchangeable.

I have been internally channeling since I was five years old. I would hear messages from angels, guides and other enlightened beings, both internally (inside my mind) and externally (outside my mind). I came to understand that channeling is very natural and I looked forward to hearing what my helpers had to say.

As I matured with my gifts and looked to others (mediums) for their guidance, I often found myself feeling confused. I would wonder why their messages were so different than the ones I received. It made me wonder if the messages I was hearing were just my imagination.

What I have come to believe and understand is that the person receiving the messages is indeed interpreting a combination of spirit sources combined with their own practical experiences. A channeler may have past issues that have not yet been released. There may be patterns of abuse, intolerance or spiritual confusion. Messages that you receive are in direct correlation to your emotional, physical and spiritual well-being.

While channeling, we are opening ourselves up for soul development and spiritual growth. Personal perceptions and beliefs can interfere with the channeled message. Sometimes the channeled message can come through harsh or painfully direct. If the information comes across hurtful and not helpful, it's okay to let it pass on by.

When opening up to learn this skill, remember that an important aspect is patience. Expecting too much too soon can cause frustration, which will slow your progress. Practicing patience and understanding will help you move forward in your development.

Steps for Mediumship

- Opening Prayer
- Bring in protection
- Open
- Ask
- Divulge Respectful Information
- Closing Prayer / Giving Thanks

Opening Prayer - Use any prayer that works for you. Remember to always give thanks in the prayer. Here is the prayer I usually open up with.

Dear Great Spirit,

I seek from your source, a clear channel, so that I may help _____ find direction on their life path and a loving message of the highest greatest good. Thank you for the gifts that I have received to help people find peace and happiness. Namaste.

Bring in Protection - Protection is key. Use a protection method that calls to you. I work with Archangel Michael every time I am opening a mediumship session. I ask him to bring his protective light ray all around me and around the person that I am reading. I ask that messages come through for the greatest good, love and light. Below is an example prayer of protection.

Archangel Michael,

I seek your protective light. I ask that the greatest good, love and light comes through in the messages. Please protect me and _____ during this message. My gratitude goes to you Archangel Michael.

Open - After I have said my prayer and brought in protection, I am ready to become an open channel to receive messages. Here is an acronym for OPEN that may be useful.

Oneness **P**urity **E**nlightenment **N**amaste

- Oneness - We are connected to all and all is connected to us.
- Purity - Coming from a place of love.
- Enlightenment - An internal state of being and understanding that is of the highest greatest good.
- Namaste - "I bow to you". This means to give honor to Spirit, loved ones and to the person you are working with.

I like to light a candle and focus on the flame as I draw in energy from candlelight. When I am open, messages come through in many ways. These messages may come through as colors, symbols, feelings, etc... Every Medium receives their information in different ways.

Ask - After I have opened up to allow spirit energy to come through, it's time to ask for messages. I do this internally and externally. Spirit energy can hear our spoken and internal requests. Ask and you shall receive.

Divulge Respectful Information - When receiving messages, it's extremely important to have love at the forefront. When relaying messages, please be kind upon interpretation. Ask yourself if the person you are giving the message to will be able to handle what is coming through. Is it useful information? Is it hurtful? Can it cause harm? Please make sure the message is of good intent. This part takes a lot of practice. Unfortunately, hurtful personal information can come through. After some practice, you will understand how to consider the source of the messages, so you will not harm the person who is receiving them.

At this point you may be wondering how to differentiate between your own thoughts and true messages from a spirited being. Please check the reference section on left brain/right brain thoughts in the back of this book for more information.

Closing Prayer/Giving Thanks - When I am finished channeling, I always give a prayer of thanks.

Channeled Messages

Below are some insights on channeling and how it works. This message was channeled by Laura Lyn in order to gain knowledge. This was channeled December 27th, 2010 at 8:00 pm

Q. How does channeling work for Laura Lyn?

A. We communicate through several channels or directions. We are physically here in her presence waiting for her to broadcast the message as she is receiving it through her state of relaxation. She is not physically asleep as we would know sleep, she is in a deep trance state that one would call hypnotism or being hypnotized. She is able to do this because the practice of meditation that she has had throughout the years. During her sleep state, we communicate with her and have communicated with her throughout her whole life.

Q. Are we all communicating while we sleep?

A. During sleep, you are communicating with many who visit and originate ideas through your emotions and through your existence. Communication varies depending on the individual. You are communicating with messengers and people through your sleep hours or sleep state. By practicing meditation, the messages will get stronger and more are aligning to you. The stronger your willingness and direction goes into that meditative state, the more beings will be aligned to you, for they will see that you are capable of receiving these messages.

Q: So if someone would like to communicate with spirit, is practice the key?

A: Yes, however, practice must be diligent. There are those on this earth that have a more natural ability and they are going to be led to do this. For others it would take a great deal of perseverance and structure to be able to attain the knowledge and insight.

Below is a sleeping trance that was channeled by Laura Lyn in order to gather information about the spirit realm. This was channeled November 9th, 2010 at 1:00 pm.

Laura: I'm asking for complete protection for Dale and I. When Dale asks questions, I am asking for clear subjects to come through and help bring information. As I'm falling asleep, I'm asking that I am protected entirely through this process. I'm asking that you come forward and bring messages through my dream state.

Q: Who's with us today?

A: Hello. We have Spotted Owl, Haley and Carmen.

Q: While in non physical existence, how does it feel to be where you are?

A: Our existence is as yours, we are free to move upon the earth plane, freely along the grass and through the trees. The difference would be the structure. While we have memories of our structure as they were, we can simply exist upon or within, meaning that the earth plane or heaven sphere, if you will, is as it was in the beginning, unadulterated by human existence. While we see and feel the structures, we are very aware that we can simply walk through, knowing that it is simply an illusion. Therefore, we are free to move forward, through, and around. This helps us to align with the simple truth that existence is within and without substance. Our truth is, we exist and are whole and complete within this spirit realm, spirit self. We are spirit connected to the universal force and place that is the high reaching sphere of what one would call God but we know as the whole existence of one.

Q: Are you considered enlightened beings or light workers on our terms? How could we relay where you are as an existence?

A: The human form of today has coined the term light worker. We simply exist in a state of our own enlightenment as individual spirits. We all have our gifts and our awareness that we see through and work through. We do not anticipate or think of these gifts as functions of a job like state, we simply move forward to learn and to accept that our teachings are learned existence. This helps us become higher frequencies of light. When we refer to light, we are referring to purity, pure essence. We are looking for our being, our spirit being, to be whole and complete while releasing any bondages that were presented in the earth realm while in our physical existence.

Q: How can we relay to people that it is possible to communicate with other realms?

A: As we were referring to on our realm or our sphere, we all learn in our unique manner how to elevate our spirits and purify that in our light. People here on the earth realm, in physical state, as individuals will learn in their own way if they expect or have the need to move forward with that communication.

Q: What can we do to help with some of the problems with the earth bound, the "ghosts"?

A: The individual that has a certain gift or cause to work with the beings, the soul beings, they are called into action and can communicate readily. Unfortunately those laymen, who only have an eager interest to see a ghost or see a spiritual figure, can inhibit the growth of the spiritual being. We search for those who are enlightened on your sphere to communicate with us, for you are elevating. For those who are here for mere entertainment, you are hurting us. We are hopeful that the light can shine. We are looking for those who care, searching for answers and direction on a spiritual meaning of existence.

We are at a place of hopefulness and even hopelessness in the same regard because there are many dying who have lost their way that are sinking into a deeper abyss within their own making. There are lost souls who have not gained the insight to release the fear, the possession of regret, and the horror of chaos of their making. They are sinking into a deeper abyss of shame, guilt and sadness. These are the ones we search for you to release and to rescue, to help, to honor. Communicate freely; open yourself to a belief that you can become friends with those that you cannot see. Understand that we hear you, we see you, feel you, and know you. As we communicate with you, you will freely see us and know us. It might be in your mind's eye. Know that we are real. We are here seeking and searching for answers for our lost ones. We are frightened. As they go deeper into that abyss state, they will be absorbed into the darkness. Some may call this darkness Hell. We are searching for those who are seeking to be aligned with light and truth that they can live, they can feel, they can be full of joy in their cellular essence. When we refer to cellular essence, we are speaking of spiritual awakening within the spiritual matter of truth and light.

Q: Is it our place to help those in need? When we're doing what people call spirit rescue or soul rejuvenation, are we helping to make a difference?

A: We are hearing you and we can assure you that if the spirit being is entertaining the thought of that force and listening to you that they are aligned to truth. Our worry is those who are evoking or not truly believing as they communicate. They are witnessing a spirit wither. It is of the utmost importance that the energy raises and aligns to total belief, one that is for the greater good.

Q: I've been attempting to speak to spirit around me. Are they hearing me and am I having the correct intensions while I'm speaking to them? Is what I'm doing correct?

A: Yes. Freely communicate. See in your mind's eye what you are gathering.

Channeled Message Exercise

1. Write down your thoughts about the channeled messages above. Were there any new concepts that you have never thought of?

_____

_____

_____

_____

_____

_____

_____

2. Did you identify with any of the concepts in the channeled messages?

_____

_____

_____

_____

_____

_____

_____

3. Write down any additional thoughts about the channeled messages.

_____

_____

_____

_____

_____

_____

_____

It's Time for You to Channel

Here are other examples of channeled messages from Laura and friends. Read the messages and then close your eyes and ask your spirit helpers to come through in writing. Allow the words to flow.

More Channeled Messages

Channeled by Laura Lyn - January 2010

Dear Ones,

Allow yourself the freedom of movement. Directionally we are at every passage to help you align and discover your highest state of being. We celebrate when you climb and ascend forward. We ascend with you as you actualize your inherent truth of beauty and principle.

Just as the solid oak trunk does not shake at the solid winds, we will never leave your field when under tension or hassle. Our strength and silent encouragement flows so you can be in motion to help the world resonate with its new shifting truth of a perfect frequency of love.

You are discovering rapidly that the state of being is the state of flowing. By allowing yourself to resonate with a life of peace, you are realigning the constitution of conditioned behaviors that has by error manifested fear and isolation. You are allowing alteration of an old way that prevented movement.

Become free and move forward in your destiny of peace,
Archangel Gabriel

Channeled by Deborah Lute - January 2011

When you lay your head to rest tonight, may you fall into a deep slumber unlike all other nights. Upon wakening, you will feel refreshed, enlightened, full of energy, and much wiser from all the information you have received during the night. Listen closely to the voices, for they are there to guide you on your path. Take heed to the gentle nudge that might send you in another direction, for it has the knowledge to know the right direction to take. Feel the Love that is inside you and let that Love guide you in all the steps you take. Release that Love into the atmosphere, it will be felt by all. Trust in me. Keep positive throughout your path, for positive brings positive back in all directions. Take just one moment every day to look deeply into yourself and know, truly know, you are special, loved, and able to project that love into the air to be felt by all.

Archangel Gabriel

Channeled by Russell Lute - January 2011

Focus on what you see
Envision and it will be
Listen to what you hear
Conquer what you fear
Strive for what is right
Look within to gain your sight
Breathe to feel alive
Nourish and you will thrive
Dream to make it real
Love so you can feel
Accept to become whole
Believe and you will know

Archangel Gabriel

Channeling Practice

Now that you have read the messages, use the space below to write your own channeled message. Remember to allow the words to flow.

_____

_____

_____

_____

_____

_____

_____

Divination and Dowsing

Definition: *Divination is the art or practice that seeks to foresee or foretell future events or discover hidden knowledge usually by the interpretation of signs or by the aid of supernatural powers.*

There are countless forms of divination used by all cultures throughout the world. We will cover some of the more common methods of divination in this section.

Pendulum

A pendulum is commonly used to get a yes or no answer. A good explanation for why a pendulum works is: "Your Higher Self influences your physical self by using minute muscles that your physical self is not aware of".

Here are some ideas to help you utilize the art of receiving answers through the use of pendulums.

- Allow your body to loosen and relax, shake out any tensions, allow your mind to empty while remaining emotionally detached and objective.
- Stabilize your posture. Take a nice deep breath and release while paying attention to your stance.
- Try to avoid preconceived notions of the forthcoming answer.
- Ask the pendulum "show me a yes", then ask "show me a no", finally ask "show me what neutral looks like".

The direction the pendulum moves is not the same for everyone. Pendulum movements are in sync with your Higher Self.

Pendulum Exercise

Pendulums can be used for more than yes or no answers. They can be used to detect energy around someone. Have someone stand still and slowly walk towards them with your pendulum. You will find that the pendulum will begin to move when you get within the range of their energy. You can use this method to "measure" the distance that a person's energy flows from their body.

What did you experience with the pendulum exercise? Write down your findings here.

_____

_____

_____

_____

_____

_____

_____

_____

Dowsing Rods

Dowsing rods basically function on the same principal as the pendulum. Your body reacts to your subconscious without your conscious knowledge. Dowsing has been in use since ancient times.

The most common usage for dowsing rods is to find water. Dowsing can be used to find lost objects, to get yes or no answers, and to find oil wells. Other uses include finding ghosts, detecting energy points, such as acupuncture points on the body, and energetic fields of all types.

For most people, the art of dowsing requires practice. Some are "naturals" who are very accurate with their skills from their first try.

A good way to practice is the same as practicing with the pendulum. Stand with your feet shoulder width apart. Ask the dowsing rods "show me a yes", and then ask "show me a no", finally ask "show me what neutral looks like".

Dowsing Rod Exercises

Walk across your yard from one end to the other with the intent of finding the water pipes coming into the house. Do this several times then mark your detected spot. Go into the house and see where the pipe actually comes into the house. Were you accurate? Describe your experience below.

_____

_____

_____

_____

_____

_____

_____

_____

_____

Have someone hide an item in your house or yard. Use one dowsing rod as a pointer and ask where the hidden item is located. See how accurately you can determine the location of the missing object.

Were you able to locate the object? Write down the details here.

_____

_____

_____

_____

_____

_____

_____

_____

_____

_____

_____

_____

Scrying

Here is a scrying definition from Wikipedia:

Scrying is the practice that involves seeing things psychically in a medium, usually for purposes of obtaining spiritual visions and more rarely for purposes of divination or fortune-telling. The media used are most commonly reflective, translucent, or luminescent substances such as crystals, stones, glass, mirrors, water, fire, or smoke. Scrying has been used in many cultures as a means of divining the past, present, or future. Although scrying is most commonly done with a crystal ball, it may also be performed using any smooth surface, such as a bowl of liquid, a pond, or a crystal.

Scrying Exercises

I consider scrying as a means of achieving a meditative state while using your eyes to actually see the messages. Below are a few exercises to help you to practice scrying.

Candle Scrying:

- Light a candle and choose a comfortable location that will allow you to look at the candle without any distractions.
- Focus on the candle and ask yes or no questions.
- Ask the flame to show you what a yes or no looks like.
- Take note of your success in receiving answers.

_____

_____

_____

_____

_____

_____

_____

_____

_____

Mirror Scrying:

- Find a room that is dark and has a mirror.
- Use a candle as your light source.
- While looking in the mirror, focus on one area of your face for no more than one to two minutes at a time.
- If the visions do not come within a couple minutes, look away, relax and try again.
- What did you see? What messages did you receive from your vision?

_____

_____

_____

_____

_____

_____

_____

_____

_____

_____

_____

Oracle Cards for Communication

Oracle Cards provide insight and positive outlook for those seeking answers to their innermost questions. When working with Oracle cards you are tapping into knowledge from angels, spirits, guides, and your higher self. Using Oracle cards on a regular basis can help you get into more conscious communication with your guides and the guides of others. Remember that practice will improve your skills over time.

Keep your intentions pure while doing a reading. I always say a prayer for the highest greatest good, highest greatest light, and the highest greatest love. This is a very powerful prayer that will help you receive the most helpful and loving guidance during your reading.

Ten Steps to an Intuitive Reading

As you work with Oracle Cards you will find that you can read them intuitively. Begin by studying each card before you read its description. Look at each card and study the color, forms, and pictures in depth. Write your answers in the journal section in the back of this book.

1. What number is on the card?

2. What does this number mean to you?

3. What comes to mind when you see this number?

4. What symbols do you see?

5. What comes to mind when you see each symbol?

6. Look very specifically at each image and note down what comes to mind.

7. Now step back from the card and look at the big picture of the card and note down what you see.

8. What do the colors tell you about the mood of the card?

9. Can you get a sense of anything else?

10. Now put your intuition to the test. Ask a question about where you are in your life right now. Pull a card and place it in front of you. Go through the above steps and tell the story to your higher self.

I have developed *Finding Your Inner Mystic* Oracle Cards that are a great tool to help you learn how to work with cards. These cards are designed to help you unlock your Inner Mystic so you can discover ancient truths that have always sustained and recently become more readily available by shifting frequencies in the cosmos.

This divine space that sees all and knows all captures truth and joy. Tapping into this space you become one with nature, beauty, and unconditional love.

Protection (Have No Fear)

Let's go over some details about protection. The most important thing to realize is that fear can be your biggest hindrance. We have dominion while in our plane of existence.

When I open a spirit circle, I always ask Archangel Michael to bring in his loving white ray of protection around the group. I also make sure the intent of the group is pure and that our intention is to help those who ask regardless of the circumstances. You can't go wrong when your true intention is pure.

Believe in yourself. Doubt is based on fear. Fear can cause you to lose confidence in your strengths. When you have lost confidence, you allow unwanted energies to resonate to you because you have unknowingly lowered your vibration to closely match lower frequency energies.

Anger also brings in doubt and fear. When you're angry you are giving energy to what has made you angry. This actually gives the source of your anger more power over you. When you give in to anger, you will begin to doubt, which brings you back to fear.

I have spoken with many people over the years and I've found that fear will bring your development to a standstill. Fear can actually take you further from your truths. It is important to remember that we have dominion over our well being. Fear alone can give unwanted energies the "permission" to alter how we feel.

For thousands of years crystals have been used for their energetic qualities. Here is a list of some crystals that I use for protection when delving into the psychic senses. The stones seem to carry with them an essence that "wards off" negativity.

Crystals for Protection

Crystal	Purpose
Blue Lace Agate	Protection and Inspiration
Moonstone	Manifesting and Protection
Snowflake Obsidian	Shielding and Protection
Amethyst	Power, Focus, Protection
Red Jasper	Protection and Grounding

These crystals are available for purchase at: www.angelreader.net. For more information on crystals, please read Crystals to Amplify the Energy in the reference section at the end of this workbook.

Clearing and Protection

When working with subtle energies, it will sometimes be necessary to clear a space. The intent of clearing is to remove negative energies. The method I use most for clearing is smudging. Smudging is often done with sage. Sage can be purchase loose or wrapped in stick form. Most area metaphysical shops carry the smudging supplies mentioned below.

Smudging a House

- An abalone shell or thick pottery will work well as a smudging bowl.
- To avoid blowing sparks out of the bowl, close doors and windows and turn off fans.
- After lighting the end of the smudge stick, allow the flame to smolder out. You may want to do this outdoors to ensure your safety. When outdoors you can use a smudge fan or gently shake the smudge stick to allow the flame to go out. After the flame is out, the smudge stick will continue to smoke.
- Fanning: A feather fan works well, but if you do not have a feather your hand will also direct the smoke nicely.
- Gently fan the smoke from the floor up towards the ceiling. Do this in a clockwise circle in each corner of your room. When you are done with the last corner, move to the center of the room, raise the bowl, and fan smoke up toward the center of the room. Smudge each room in the house the same way.
- It is important to remember to be safe during the smudging process. It is not recommended to leave sage burning unattended.

I always say the following words - *Thank you Great Spirit for bringing protection and honor to this space. Archangel Michael, we are asking for your assistance to bring your light forward to protect this room and space, only allowing the highest essences in. We are grateful for your protective ray. Let it be.*

Smudging Yourself

- Start at the ground and gently fan the smoke upward. Work your way up until you send the smoke up above your head.
- The smoke represents prayers and also acts as a carrying agent for lower frequencies to rise up and out of a space.

Review What You've Learned

This is a good time to review what you have learned in the first two chapters by reflecting on the ABC's. Write down your experiences that are related to the statements below. How have your views changed since you began chapter one?

Awareness - Awareness of who you are.

_____

_____

_____

_____

_____

_____

_____

_____

Belief – Trust the information that your intuition is giving you.

_____

_____

_____

_____

_____

_____

_____

Courage –Have the courage to ask, feel, discern, and speak.

_____

_____

_____

_____

_____

_____

_____

_____

_____

A Look at the Third Chapter......

In chapter three you will learn about ghosts, spirits, guides and enlightened beings. You will also learn ways to help earthbound spirit energies. This chapter is also designed to teach basic methods of energy discernment.

Chapter Three

∞

Spirit Rescue / Soul Rejuvenation

Discerning is Key

If it feels, smells, tastes, or looks bad it most likely is! Nasty people here on earth who have passed are likely to be nasty ghosts on the other side as well. If it feels wrong to be in an area get away. I would not recommend "testing the energies." Trust your instinct. In chapter two, we discussed how to connect with earth bound energies and how to trust the messages that are coming through. In this chapter, we will use what we've learned to help earth bound energies move forward on their journey.

Spirit Rescue - What I Have Come to Believe

The first time I heard the term Spirit Rescue, I was puzzled by the use of the word "rescue." I questioned why someone would believe we can rescue spirits. Why would a spirit need my help? Couldn't spirits communicate readily with other spirits? I have learned that many "earthbound" spirits are not able to understand that they have passed. Some spirits may actually hear people much easier than they can hear other spirits because they have not released their attachment to their physical existence.

The first thing to understand about Spirit Rescue is that there are no absolutes. My beliefs have been in line with my experiences, as much as yours will be with your own. Everyone has different paths, beliefs and religious personal truths. The same goes for ghosts who are seeking help.

Many people practice spirit rescue by sending spirits to "the light," as if it were a place. I have come to believe that the light is actually an eternal source of joy that is connected to Great Spirit (God). I feel as soon as the ghost remembers who he or she is and connects with their source of joy, then a great light shines within and without. In that space, truth is revealed and release can and will happen. The spirit is able to release past regrets, untruths, anger, sadness and fear. Darkness is replaced with the light of unconditional love.

There are many ways people find their own light. How do we help them if they're seeking assistance? The answer is very simple. We communicate with them. Whether or not they can fully understand or comprehend is anybody's guess. The point is we do the best that we can and hope that our help brings release to the spirit seeking assistance.

Who exactly are we helping? Earthbound spirits (ghosts) are people who have passed on and are unable to move forward. Sometimes they chose to stay at this earthbound level because of fear. An earthbound spirit may feel that they will lose touch with a loved one, so they choose not to transcend. Ghosts may have an attachment to something here on the Earth such as a home or car. There are as many reasons why a spirit chooses to stay earthbound or loses their way as there are ways to help.

Here are three types of spirits that I have worked with:

1. Lost Spirits
2. Angry Spirits
3. Trapped Spirits

Lost Spirits

A lost spirit is a person who is out of touch with their reality. They may not realize they have passed on and because of their confusion; they are functioning in a dream like state. Existing in this state of mind can be frustrating because they feel helpless and alone. This type of spirit may move and shuffle furniture or knock on walls. This is unsettling for someone to hear these noises with no known source.

When I am trying to figure out how to help a spirit, I ask open ended questions. When the answers come in muffled I am aware that the ghost is the lost (dreamy) type. The answers may be confusing or make no sense at all. Think about it, when you are dreaming do the surroundings fit with your everyday waking experience? Dreams are highly symbolic. This is how ghosts speak when they are in the dreamy state. They show things that are important in their life in rapid cessation. I may get flashes of different material goods or see scenes of a work / home environment. When you come upon a "dreamy spirit", it may be difficult to convey to them that they are indeed dead and without their physical body.

Next I ask more direct questions of the spirit. Are you aware that you are no longer alive on this Earth? Do you remember how you died? I try to jolt them "awake" as lovingly as I can. I do not want to add to their confusion in any way. Eventually the spirit becomes aware of their condition. I then have the opportunity to guide them through their light path. I use spirit guidance to help them find their light. This light may be within or it may be an actual place, which depends on their beliefs and past experiences.

Angry Spirits

Everyone knows somebody who is extremely angry at life. Angry people tend not to have many friends and may have alienated themselves from their family. I feel sorrow for these people because they are hurting and very lonely. The problem is how in the world do you help them? Most of us certainly do not want their angry wrath upon ourselves. It seems easier to tip toe around the person in hopes of not being seen or heard.

When a ghost is angry, he or she may become violent. While I have not had many of these experiences, I did have one incidence that was violent. I was at the Mansfield Reformatory when I came upon a very angry sprit who didn't like women. I began to communicate with this mean spirited ghost. He was upset that I was on his turf and he let me know by cursing. I tried to reason with him, but he told me to get out. When I left the area I was told "if you come back we will do battle".

I explained everything to a volunteer staff member who in turn told others about the encounter. Unfortunately, one of them did not believe my story. He wanted proof and a better idea of where this occurred. I felt a little put off and proceeded to "prove" my experience.

I practically ran to the spot where I left the fuming spirit and found myself in total darkness. The room where my experience occurred was called the toilet room. There were rows of replacement sinks and toilets along the aisles. I slowed down and realized I was brushing up against a fence on my right side. I checked myself and in that instance felt a pressure on my back. I remember clearly thinking someone is going to get seriously hurt. I had a flash of horror run through my mind because I was sure someone was falling onto me. I was brutally pushed into the porcelain sinks and toilets that were at my left. I felt instant pain and realized quickly that my hands were wet. Flashlights beamed at me from onlookers across the room. I looked down and saw blood dripping from my hands. I could hardly walk because of the intense pain in my right knee.

Despite the labored efforts of walking I continued to go towards the steps where I found the mean entity earlier. I yelled "Why did you do this? Where are you?" He was nowhere in sight. He proved his point, he did not want me on his turf and he had warned me. He won the battle and I learned a lesson that I thought I already knew. Never let your ego get the best of you when doing this work. If you are being told you don't belong, listen. That was a hard learned lesson and I will always thank him for teaching me. I pray for him to find happiness but I will not walk into his turf again.

So what happens if you run across a brutal type who is determined to get you away from their "home"? My answer is you oblige them if they are not causing immediate harm. If they are harming people you may need to take action. Some circumstances will require additional assistance. While I do not enjoy working with angry spirits, I will do what is needed to make sure everyone is safe.

When working with angry spirits, I always have others in the area to make sure that I am safe. I ask questions and try to understand where they are coming from. If I realize that there are no alternatives, I will ask my spiritual helpers to "usher" the dangerous entity to a safer place. I have no idea where this safer place is, but I know it's somewhere away from those who are in harm's way. I have had many people call or write to let me know how nice it is to live in peace again.

The spiritual helpers I am referring to are the angels that I work with. When doing this work, it's important to find out who your spiritual helpers are. It's not required to know your guidance by name, just know that you're not alone. You may call upon spirit guidance at any time to assist. I believe these beings have dominion when asked to assist us.

If you don't feel confident that the spirit entity is gone please don't hesitate to seek additional help. It's a good idea to network with people in this field. It's always beneficial to learn by exchanging ideas. When outside assistance is needed, it's important to work with someone you know and feel comfortable with. When working with others, it's vital to leave your ego or any personal opinions out of this work.

After working with an angry spirit I always perform a cleansing. I use prayer, Angel Ray's, and sage to clear the area. If I am sure the residence is cleansed, I will cast a circle of sea salt around the premises. Be careful of this because the salt can work both ways. Salt is a barrier. We don't want to "lock in" spirits, we want to keep the unwanted spirits out.

Trapped Spirits

Have you ever felt trapped? Think back, were you ever in a relationship that was not working any longer? When you lived in that space it was most likely draining and frustrating. You may have pondered ways to leave without hurting the other person. You could have felt hopeless and dissatisfied.

Perhaps you have felt trapped at a work place. Every moment at the job may feel like a prison of sorts. You must be on the job to earn a living but your heart isn't in it and your spirit seems "locked up". There is no room to grow to your highest potential when you feel trapped.

There are many reasons why a spirit may be trapped. The spirit may be reluctant to leave because they don't want to lose touch with loved ones here on earth. They essentially trap themselves. There are also sprits, often children who want to move on but stronger spirits keep them at bay. The stronger spirits may do this because they are afraid of being alone or have a need to be in control. Yes, spirits can be control freaks. A strong spirit who is not ready to transcend will often take hostages.

There are many ways to work through this plight. The first thing to do is get the story and go from there. Why is the ghost trapped? What kind of help is needed? It's fascinating what can happen with patience, diligence and stubbornness. Don't give up, eventually more will be revealed and the trapped spirit may find their inner peace.

Soul Rejuvenation – Messages from Spirit

Below is a channeled message that was recorded the night after a spirit circle on December 29th, 2010 at 10 pm. This message is included here to provide more details on how "spirit rescue" works and why it is important.

Q: We had a spirit circle last night and some of us felt there were many more in line waiting for their turn.

A: You are correct that there are many souls in line looking for revival. While there were many more there, they will continue to be at that space. The reason for our cry out for circles is there are many layers that are affected and receiving help from these circles. Please understand that while you saw several people receiving light, receiving inner light, there were many more that you were not aware of that were receiving that light in tandem. There are many more that understand and move forward. There will always be more waiting and searching and understanding. There was no harm done closing the circle at an earlier time. Please understand that there is always time and perfection in all.

Excerpt from Helping Ghosts:

Spirits in the Material

My friend, Louis Charles just released *Helping Ghosts* which covers spirit rescue in a refreshing, loving way. Louis Charles has assisted in teaching *Soul Rejuvenation/Spirit Rescue* several times so I thought this would be a perfect fit for this part of the workbook. I got permission to include the following excerpts from his book, *Helping Ghosts - A Guide to Understanding Lost Spirits*. These insights are another excellent way to get a well rounded view of what spirit rescue is about.

My awakening to spirit did not happen at church but at home one day. The strong presence stayed with me for about a week, and I felt an intense love, peace, and joy associated with it. More importantly, I also awoke to a voice submerged within my heart that accompanied the tangible, spirit presence. I can only equate this voice with being a "knowing inside me." As I quieted the thoughts of my mind, I could hear the voice much better; therefore, meditation became my path toward recognizing what emanated from within my deepest being.

My mind was numb with the ideas that were filling it, and I could only wonder about my former, religious beliefs of people being eternally lost, separated from each other due to their sins. I no longer could believe in a fiery place of punishment. The fear of Hell was dead in me. I wondered what happens to those who are full of hatred, anger, condemnation, worthlessness and other forms of suffering. Where do they go after their bodies expire? Wouldn't they also be a part of this peaceful spirit energy I experienced? If so, how could they remain in a state of torment? I wanted answers. If people did continue to suffer, how could that be possible? Where would they suffer? The questions kept filling my head.

I began searching my heart concerning the fate of humanity after my spiritual awakening. This is when I began visualizing what I suspected could be occurring with a part of mankind. When a body dies, I realized the person could remain temporarily lost, especially if they were not aware of their higher self. I theorized that hurting people might unwittingly choose to stay on a path of suffering. Becoming lost was not a condition produced from having an informed choice, and it was not a judgment emanating from a condemning god. It was like being adrift at sea, unaware of where to go or how to navigate home. Someone needed to be a beacon and shine light in order to bring the abandoned to shore, to aid the lost from their disorientation. We often see people around us who need guidance. Why wouldn't disembodied human souls possibly need guidance, too? I realized that the state of not knowing who we truly are is hell. People do not have to die in order to experience hell, for hell is not a place of suffering but a state of mind. If some people are pained by emotional trauma today, are we to believe that the death of their body will instantly heal their mind?

The belief that the human spirit survives death of the physical body is found within most religions, but not every faith teaches the existence of ghosts or how to help them. It is interesting that Judaism, Buddhism, and Hinduism have teachings about ghosts; that they are suffering human spirits. Interestingly, it is taught by certain sects within these religions that suffering souls often need our help to move beyond their emotional trauma. Yet within Western society, our culture has not readily embraced the idea of ghosts being impaired, human spirits whom we can help. We seem unaware of this idea. It would appear we prefer to view ghosts from a frightening perspective, or we simply do not want to know they exist at all.

Soul Rejuvenation - Exercise One

Reflect on the previous excerpt and answer the questions below.

1. What details made sense to you?

_____

_____

_____

_____

_____

_____

_____

_____

_____

2. Have you ever felt anything similar to what Louis was experiencing?

_____

_____

_____

_____

_____

_____

_____

_____

3. What are your thoughts on spirit rescue (soul rejuvenation)?

_____

_____

_____

_____

_____

_____

_____

_____

_____

Excerpt from Helping Ghosts:
There is no Other Side

I became intuitively aware that our ability to create and become trapped within our own illusions of past and future is something that does not necessarily dissipate simply due to death of the physical body. It is a commonly-held belief by many that when a person dies they leave the earth and their former life behind without any strings attached. Due to certain religious teachings, there are those who strongly think that the grave is an impenetrable wall between the quick and the dead. Despite what others choose to believe, it eventually became apparent to me that ghost sightings are evidence that refutes this idea. I could no longer assume that every deceased person progresses directly unto another place. Numerous accounts of disembodied spirits of people, who have remained behind after their physical body expired, reveal that ghosts display a strong attachment to their past, something obviously enforced by the power of their mind. Even though ghosts might not be trapped within a specific, past event, it is certainly prior life experience on earth that still enslaves them. Like many, I felt it was possible for disincarnate spirits to have unfinished business they strongly feel needs to be resolved. Yet, I also suspected some might fear saying goodbye to loved ones, not wanting to face an uncertain future. Even though the reasons for remaining behind on earth likely differ from one ghost to another, I eventually came to the conviction that every ghost is fundamentally living within a false, psychologically-constructed prison. Some are simply lost within their mind more than others. I theorized that ghosts are characteristically haunted by different forms of fear based upon their past experiences, keeping them to some extent disconnected from their own present moment.

Channeled Message on Soul Rejuvenation

Here is an excerpt from a message that Laura Lyn channeled on April 12th, 2010 at 9 pm regarding Spirit Rescue (Soul Rejuvenation).

Q: Is the chaos in the spirit realm affecting our realm? And spirit rescue will help all realms?

A: Yes there are three realms that are directly affected by untruths. We are affecting the realm of the dead, the undead and the unborn. The unborn of the future are waiting for the dead to receive the light so they can come into this sphere. The unborn, the souls to take place and harbor their step and beauty on this earth, cannot and will not take their step until the dead, the earthen dead, are released and find their light.

Q: I have found that love is "contagious". When we do spirit rescue work, is it the same? Is spirit rescue something that can spread and help many?

A: Yes it does. A great light shines. There are many souls that you are unaware of that are in line for this truth. A great cathedral opens its doorways when we speak of love and enlightenment.

Soul Rejuvenation - Exercise Two

1. Reflect on the previous material and write your answers to the questions below. What details in this section rang true for you?

_____

_____

_____

_____

_____

_____

_____

_____

_____

_____

_____

_____

_____

2. Did you disagree with any outlook presented?

_____

_____

_____

_____

_____

_____

_____

3. Write down your thoughts on spirit rescue as if you were explaining the subject to someone who has never heard of it.

_____

_____

_____

_____

_____

_____

_____

_____

Soul Rejuvenation Discussion

Have you developed any new insights about Soul Rejuvenation after reading this chapter? List anything that comes to mind below.

_____

_____

_____

_____

_____

_____

_____

_____

_____

_____

_____

_____

_____

A Look at the Fourth Chapter......

In the next chapter we will learn about paranormal investigations. Everything you have learned up to this point will be useful.

Chapter Four

∞

Paranormal Investigation

This chapter is intended to give you a brief introduction to paranormal investigating. Investigations are a good opportunity to bring compassion and respect to earthbound energies.

There is no need to fear while investigating. Always go into an investigation with love and compassion. If you are feeling stressed or depressed you should not be involved in a paranormal investigation.

I am a psychic investigator for a paranormal group based in Akron, Ohio called S.I.G.H.T. Below is a description of what the group believes about paranormal investigations. More information can be found on www.sightofohio.com

Spiritual Insight Ghost Hunting Team is a group of spiritual investigators from Akron, Ohio. We don't feel the need to prove that ghosts exist. We already believe and accept the fact that there are energies among us that can't be easily seen or interpreted. Our team supports spiritual means to contact these energies.

We feel that a ghost hunt should be conducted with the utmost respect and compassion because "ghosts" are actually people that do not have a physical existence. We have encountered earthbound energies that ask for help because they are caught up in their past concerns while they were in the physical realm.

Spirit Rescue is a process, it's not for entertainment and it is not to be taken lightly. It is a means to help those who are lost, frightened, maybe extremely angry, perhaps resentful... We get to the bottom of their story and identify how we can help.

Paranormal Investigation Etiquette

- **Minimize noise** – It is good practice to keep noise to a minimum during an investigation. Other investigators may be recording or attempting to quiet their mind to see what comes through.
- **Do not whisper** - While quiet is extremely important during an investigation, it is also important to not whisper. Whispering can cause false positives in audio data. If

you need to speak, always speak at your normal conversational volume. It is best to keep all talking to a minimum.

- **Make written notes of your perceptions** - There are many benefits to keeping communication to a minimum during your investigation. Writing your observation as it occurs will make for stronger evidence after the investigation is over. Make sure you note the time and place for each entry. The occurrence will have more merit when it's compared with other investigators notes; especially if they mention the same or similar experiences.

- **Do not smoke** - Particles in cigarette smoke can carry much farther than we are able to detect with our naked eye but often result in false mists in photographs.

- **Do not wear perfume** - It is thought that floral scents are a signal of the presence of spirits.

- **Keep your flashlight pointed at the ground** - This is often overlooked at an investigation where there are many investigators. A flashlight beam can cause someone to be temporarily blinded and also cause false positives in photos.

Paranormal Investigation Terms

The following is a list which includes ghost hunting terms and definitions from our friend Louis Charles who owns angelsghosts.com.

- **Anomaly** - Something found on a picture, photograph, video or voice recording that has no explainable source.

- **Apparition** - A spirit that is in human form and usually visible to the naked eye; or may appear in a photo undetected originally by the naked eye.

- **Cameras** - Paranormal investigators use both digital and 35mm cameras. Digital cameras are great because they seem more adept at capturing anomalies and give instant results. They are also cheaper to use than film.

- **Digital voice recorder** – It's a good idea to record everything while on an investigation. When you play back what you have recorded you may discover some EVP's.

- **Dowsing rods** - Dowsing is a good way to locate energy or spirits. You can also ask questions and receive answers.

- **Ectoplasm** - The term used for a smoke like or fog looking mist that appears in photos but was not discernible by the human eye. This phenomenon has been captured in the midst of large groups of people, as well.

- **EMF Meter** - A meter for measuring electromagnetic fields. Spirits have been found to interrupt or even create their own electromagnetic fields. Compasses can also be used to detect changes in EMF's. A spike in EMF activity could represent spirit activity and is an excellent tool of the paranormal investigator to locate areas to study and compare evidence of the presence of ghosts.

- **Energy Lights** - These show up on photos as colored lights during some manifestations of hauntings. They usually are not visible to the naked eye and can appear in different colors such as red, orange or green. Another word for this is orbs.

- **EVP** - "Electronic Voice Phenomenon" is the recording of audio tapes at a suspected haunted site; and although no voices were heard at the time of the recording, unexplained voices may be discovered during playback of the audio tape. Both digital recorder and traditional tape recorders may be used.

- **Flashlight** - You will be in some dark places. I put this here because it's a common item that is forgotten.

- **Ghost Box** - This is a modified digital radio that scans all the frequencies in the AM and FM band. When used with a digital recorder you may be able to capture spirit messages.

- **Infrared Camera** - Digital cameras have a filter that blocks infrared light. With a few modifications, a camera can allow only infrared light. This makes a great night vision camera.

- **Intelligent Haunting** - When spirits dwell in a specific area and demonstrate an interaction with those here in the physical realm.

- **Kinetic Energy** - Description for the movement of objects by a ghost. A physical manifestation of an unseen force which may move, throw or even destroy objects. These ghosts are referred to as "Poltergeists".

- **Motion Sensors and Detectors** - Some paranormal investigators use motion detectors to watch for unseen objects or infrared (heat) movement.

- **Orb** - Orbs are believed to be energy or the spirit and soul of individuals, which show up as circles or balls of light in photos - varying in size, color and opacity. As a side note, it is important to know that dust, rain or snow, directly in front of the camera can also appear to be orbs in a photograph.

- **Pendulum** - You can communicate with spirits and receive answers while using the pendulum.
- **Plasma** - Moving orbs caught during the time of camera exposure. Orbs have also been filmed moving, on video. In photos they appear as streaking light or as an orb with a tail showing the path of motion. These are also known as "supercharged orbs" in motion.
- **Poltergeist** - German for "noisy ghost." These ghosts manifest in the physical enough to produce sounds and the movement of objects. See Kinetic Energy.
- **Residual Haunting** - When a spirit is seen doing the same thing over and over, many believe this to be simply an energy imprint or residual haunting. Usually these spirits do not interact with those who see them.
- **Shadow People / Dark Shadows** - Unexplainable dark shadows in photos and video which sometimes may be seen with the naked eye.
- **Thermal Scanners/Thermometers** - Used to detect cold or hot spots which can indicate paranormal activity.
- **Vortex** - A long streak across a photo that may be caused by a very high-speeding "orb;" some believe vortices are a gateway between both realms (physical and spirit realms). They are usually white in color and may appear as a funnel shape. Camera straps, human hair, a tree branch, etc., right in front of the camera lens during exposure have been notoriously mistaken for a vortex. It is important to make sure anything that may interfere with your photo is removed from within the front of the camera.

Where to get Paranormal Investigation Equipment

The Fringe Tech Store owned by Louis Charles is an excellent source for electronic paranormal research equipment. You can see his products at: http://www.angelsghostsforum.com/fringe_tech_ghost_hunting_store.

Electronic Voice Phenomenon

Electronic voice phenomena, also known as EVP, are recordings of spirit voices. Usually the voices are not heard during the recording session. In order to find EVP's the recording is analyzed after the ghost hunt. Software can be used to analyze the recording and to clarify the voices. Audacity is a popular program used by ghost hunting groups. Audacity is a free program that can be found online at: http://audacity.sourceforge.net

Conclusion – Summing it Up

Let's face it, paranormal investigation has become very trendy over the last years. If you are reading this you are most likely in a sub group who takes communicating and working with spirit very seriously. I have seen spirits most of my life and I have come to a conclusion that it is very natural to interact with beings that are of the spirit world.

The most important part of questing in the spirit world through any type of investigation process is respect and compassion. I would not like it if a stranger came into my home with a flashlight asking for me to bump a wall or make a noise. It's much kinder to explain why we're here, that we mean no harm, and we are interested in getting to know you. I seldom go on a ghost hunt just for pure proof. I am usually at a location seeing if a person who has passed on needs assistance. Please understand that spirit energy is everywhere. There are places all over the world where spirit energy (people) are looking for help.

I do need to warn you, there is also dark energy waiting for a vulnerable moment. I was attacked badly at the Mansfield Reformatory. It was when I let my shields down and I wanted to "prove" I was talking with a mean spirited entity. I was told by this entity not to return, but I did. My ego got in the way. Never allow your ego to influence you at a ghost hunt. This could be potentially dangerous. Keep respectful and highly shielded. If you keep the rule of thumb to do no harm (don't provoke), you will keep safe and the lower energies will leave you alone. Lower energies have no interest in bothering people who carry this type of principle. Always keep safe and follow compassion from your heart chakra and all will be well.

Enjoy this work and know you are helping real people find their way to peace. Light equals love, that's the answer to everything. When a ghost finds their light they are finding love, and that energy is a great source that is connected to all. Ghosts are only dead when they do not see this light. Once you help them see the light within their inner essence, they are free to evolve and move forward in a frequency of peace. Only they can make the decision to release their past and fears. You have the potential to assist them in finding their truth that will help them remember who they are.

Good luck and remember the light!
Blessings and peace,
Laura Lyn

Further Reference

Signs That You're Evolving Spiritually

I call evolving spiritually the Internal Spiritual Shift. Below are some examples of what many of my students and friends have experienced.

- You start seeing things dart around in the corner of your eyes. It may sometimes be colors, orbs or even life forms.
- Singing or humming to yourself for seemingly no reason.
- Increased desire to help people.
- Ears ringing or a high pitch shhhhhhhhhh sound.
- Feeling the presence of someone beside of you.
- Giving away items of value to thrift stores or people in need.
- Starting to see things more globally.
- Smelling flowers or sweet scents when there aren't any around.
- Having dreams about angels, spirit guides or loved ones.
- Becoming highly sensitive to loud music or noises.
- Violent or distasteful television shows have no place in your life any longer.
- Becoming interested in cultures around the world.

Left Brain / Right Brain Thoughts

We were born with hemispheres, left brain/right brain. The left side of the brain is where logic comes from. This is your learned experiences from the past. The right side is the creative side. This is where you visualize and interpret. Below is an exercise that you can practice on your own. When internally answering the questions below, listen to where the information is coming from.

- What color are your eyes?
- Where were you born?
- What was your first pet's name?
- Do you have siblings?
- Where do you work?

Now visualize a trip that you would love to take. Close your eyes and picture the vacation spot. Feel the space where this picture is coming from. Below is a chart to help you further understand the differences between left brain/right brain thinking.

Left Brain	Right Brain
Chronological	Random
Logical	Intuitive
Analytical	Unsystematic
Fact Based	Imagination
Objective	Subjective
Looks at parts	Looks at wholes

Crystals to Amplify the Energy

Crystals amplify physical, mental, emotional, and spiritual energy. I constantly work with crystals when delving into the spirit realms. My work would not be the same without them. Using crystals significantly increases clarity. This clarity will help you become more open and depending on the crystals, more grounded.

What Crystals Should I Use?

There are many opinions on the function of crystals and their purposes. Below is a list of crystals that will help to enhance your psychic abilities by balancing your chakras. If you focus too much on one area and not another, you could have undesirable results. Balance is one of the main factors that should be monitored closely by you during this time of growth and development.

Chakra Balancing Crystals		
Chakra	**Purpose**	**Crystal**
Crown	Focus	Amethyst
Third Eye	Inspiration	Blue Aventurine
Throat	Communication	Sodalite
Heart	Harmony	Green Aventurine
Solar Plexus	Wisdom	Citrine
Sacral	Creativity and Balance	Carnelian
Root	Devotion and Grounding	Red Tiger Eye

Cleansing Your Crystals

When you buy crystals, keep in mind that crystals transmit and receive energy. If someone was sad or angry when they had anything to do with a crystal, that energy will be imprinted on the crystal. You may feel that a particular crystal isn't "right" for you because you feel this imprinted energy. This is why it is vital to cleanse or clear your crystals. Each crystal should be cleansed before use to clear any stored imprints.

Your crystals will eventually need to be cleansed again. The time between each cleansing will vary depending on the type of work you do with your crystals and how you feel about the energy that may be stored within them. I have listed several methods that I like to use for clearing crystals below.

- *Soaking: Soak the crystal in one teaspoon sea salt per quart of spring water in a glass bowl. Soak from 15 minutes to one full day depending upon how many people have touched the stone. Rinse under cool water and allow to dry.
- Lunar: Place your crystals outside during the full moon or new moon all night.
- *Solar: Place your crystals outside in full sunshine all day.
- *Burying: Wrap the crystal in cotton, silk, or linen and bury it for at least 24 hours.
- Smoke: Native Americans traditionally perform crystal cleansing using sage. Light the sage and allow the crystals to pass through the smoke.

- **Sound:** Sound vibration can be used to cleanse a group of crystals. Place the crystals in a singing bowl, tap the bowl and allow the note to resonate through the stones.
- **Prayer:** hold your crystal between both hands and ask that all the energy be cleared for the greatest good.

*NOTE: Please research your particular crystal. All crystals are not suitable for contact with water, salt, moisture, or direct sunlight.

Charging Your Crystals

After cleansing your crystals, it's good practice to charge them. Your intent and energy will be imprinted in the crystal. Your crystals came from Mother Earth. It's best to charge your crystals outdoors while honoring the earth.

Hold your crystal in your non dominant hand. Breathe deeply and visualize the energy you wish to place within your crystal. Allow it to move through your hand, down your arm to the ground. Now bring the energy back up from the earth to your crystal. Raise your dominant hand in the air and read out loud the following statement.

Great Spirit and Mother Earth,

Thank you for the energies you provide. Thank you for making this crystal in it's perfected state. Thank you for bringing the perfected elements into this crystal. Thank you Mother Earth for this crystal that has come from you. I honor you and seek to walk in beauty. So let it be.

Again breathe deeply and appreciate the beauty of everything Mother Earth and the universe provides by acknowledging and giving thanks.

Working with Candles

It was explained to me from a spirit guide, that candles pulsate light vibrations. While the candle is lit it is a literal perpetual prayer. I write the names of angels and people that I am praying for into the wax to send blessings. I write in the wax with a pen, pencil or a toothpick. I am still amazed at the comments from friends and clients about healings and prosperous manifestations that take place after candle work. When I'm finished working with a candle, I always snuff it out. I do not blow out the flame. This is giving the candlelight honor and respect.

Below is a chart of candle colors and their uses. This is a general guideline, if you feel another color would work; by all means trust your inner guidance.

Color	Purpose	Angels
White	Represents all colors. Spiritual enlightenment, cleansing, purity, clarity and unity.	Archangel Michael
Purple	Abundance, psychic powers, meditation, spirituality, protection, divination, enhances psychic ability and contact with the spirit world.	Archangel Zadkiel
Indigo	Intuition, faith, higher view.	Archangel Raziel
Blue	Communication, peace, calm, wisdom, understanding, protection, harmony and inspiration.	Archangel Michael
Green	Healing, abundance, growth, physical healing and health.	Archangel Raphael
Yellow	Intellect, inspiration, creativity, concentration, memory, logic, truth, stability and security.	Fortunata
Orange	Cleanses negative attitudes, happiness, courage and ambition.	Metatron
Red	Energy, vitality, strength, passion, love, protection, desire and action.	Archangel Chamuel

Opening the Chakras

The Chakras are areas of the body that receive (and transmit) energy. These energy centers have an interconnected influence on everything about us. Chakra is a Sanskrit word that translates as "wheel" or "turning". Chakras can be referred to as a spinning wheel like energy vortex that is associated with a specific color and energetic vibrational frequency throughout your body.

This chapter has a good overview of the seven major chakras. The material here can help you get in touch with and attune your major energy fields. You will learn about how the chakras relate to crystal, color, element, and influences.

Meditation is a good way to balance your chakras and learn about the energy and intent of the frequencies. The meditation exercises are designed to help you tune in to your chakras. Use the journal section in the back of this book to record your meditation experiences.

Crown Chakra

Crystal: Amethyst for opening
Color: Violet
Element: Thought
Influences: Pineal gland, regulates natural body rhythms

Visualize bright violet light glowing from the universe down towards and into the top of your head. This violet light connects you to the highest consciousness of truth. This truth brings deep realizations that you are never alone; in fact you are connected to all. In this truth love is the supreme essence. In this essence there comes a realization that loving oneself is essential in order to move forward. With this a new deep desire arrives to then help others. A magnificent welling pours through your system. You will feel a new need to bring your gifts and magic forward to promote happiness and peace to the world. When tapping into this light your ministry is realized and all is well. Oneness is conceptualized though this life changing process of self realization.

You are mind, body and spirit. The Crown Chakra is the epicenter of all consciousness. In this space all truth exists. Allowing yourself the acceptance and belief that God (Grand Orderly Direction) exists inside your mind, body and spirit, you will come upon the realization that you are one with the universe.

Crown Chakra Meditation

- Light a purple candle and allow the light of the flame to represent the light of your Crown Chakra.
- Close your eyes, take some deep breaths and visualize the violet light radiating upwards, and outwards spanning and webbing the universe. When you can "see" the violet light, open your eyes.
- Write down your visions as you see yourself in five years, ten years and twenty years.
- Now describe yourself as if you were looking at yourself through the eyes of the universe.
- Write down what it feels like to know you are connected to all and all is connected to you.
- Write your intentions on how to better connect with your brothers and sisters of the world.

Third Eye Chakra

Crystal: Blue Aventurine for clarity
Color: Indigo
Element: Light
Influences: Pituitary gland, influences growth and hormones

The Indigo light of this chakra rests slightly above the eyebrows at the center of the forehead. The third eye helps us focus on significant decision making. This is the central doorway to inward knowledge. The knowledge received comes from directions universally and internally. We can tap stronger into this knowledge by widening and nourishing the third eye. It is very helpful to take time to "nourish" the third eye daily by giving yourself permission to relax and be still.

Third Eye Chakra Meditation

- Light a deep blue candle and allow the light of the flame to represent the light of your Third Eye.
- Close your eyes take some deep breaths and visualize the indigo light from the universe flooding inwards. With each breath visualize the indigo shade deepening. When you can "see" the indigo (deep blue) light, open your eyes.

- Write down your last great inspiration (the latest ah ha moment). Describe the conditions and the feeling that took place when this inspiration came through.
- Now close your eyes and say thank you to your Higher Self for the realizations that came through.

Throat Chakra

Crystal: Sodalite for Communication
Color: Blue
Element: Sound
Influences: Thyroid, controls metabolism

The blue spinning energy focused into the throat aligns us to discover truth. This vortex energy system is all about authenticity. The Throat Chakra is where we communicate both verbally and nonverbally. Part of speaking truthfully involves carefully considering our words and the effect they will have once they have been spoken. We are in constant conscious flowing action between our throat chakra and higher self. A healthy throat chakra is known by the way one uses their voice. By being respectful yet clear in expressing our wants or desires to others we are aware that the state of truth is within.

Throat Chakra Meditation

- Light a blue candle and allow the light of the flame to represent the light of your Throat Chakra.
- Close your eyes take some deep breaths and visualize the blue light from the universe enveloping and moving within your Throat Chakra. With each breath visualize the blue shade warming. When you can "see" the blue light open your eyes.
- Take some time and remember the last thoughtful conversation you had. Write down your part of the conversation and how you felt.
- Now remember the last time you said the words "I love you". Write down the feeling. Were you comfortable saying the words? Did they flow freely?
- Take yourself back to the last argument you had with someone. How did it feel? Be as descriptive as possible.
- Now read over what you wrote and give your higher self thanks for helping you to interpret truths about yourself.

Heart Chakra

Crystal: Green Aventurine for healing
Color: Green
Element: Air
Influences: Thymus, helps build immune system

When the Heart Chakra is balanced, you feel love and compassion for all (including yourself). Once you are able to be kind to yourself, kindness will naturally be shared with others. Unconditional love for everything brings forth the understanding that we are all connected. When you are in this place of pure love, you will radiate that feeling throughout the universe.

Heart Chakra Meditation

- Light a green candle and allow the light of the flame to represent the light of your Heart Chakra.
- Close your eyes take some deep breaths and visualize the green light from the universe flooding inwards. With each breath visualize the green shade deepening. When you can "see" the green light, open your eyes.
- Think about love. Write down any words that come to mind. Look at those words and consider your reasons for choosing them.
- Now close your eyes and say thank you to your Higher Self for the realizations that came through.

Solar Plexus Chakra

Crystal: Citrine for wisdom
Color: Yellow
Element: Fire
Influences: Pancreas, controls digestion

This yellow power center is the gateway to self. Located just above the navel area, the Solar Plexus Chakra also aligns with your history. When this chakra is attuned, we feel empowered to create a rewarding life. You will have the ability and strength to achieve your hopes and dreams.

Solar Plexus Chakra Meditation

- Light a yellow candle and allow the light of the flame to represent the light of your Solar Plexus.
- Close your eyes. Take some deep breaths and visualize the yellow light from the universe flooding inwards. With each breath visualize the yellow shade deepening. When you can "see" the yellow light, open your eyes.
- Think about your perception of you. Write down everything you can think of that makes you who you are.
- Now take a good look at yourself through the eyes of someone you have never met. Imagine meeting someone for the first time.
- Write down what you think this person would have to say about you.
- Read what you wrote, then close your eyes and say thank you to your Higher Self for the realizations that came through.

Sacral Chakra

Crystal: Carnelian for creativity, balance
Color: Orange
Element: Water
Influences: Kidneys, adrenals

This calming orange energy is located in your lower abdomen, right below the navel. The Sacral Chakra is associated with health, pleasure, and emotions. When this chakra is balanced, you will know that you are deserving of all the happiness and comfort that life has to offer. Learning to accept and express your feelings will keep your emotional, as well as physical body healthy.

Sacral Chakra Meditation

- Light an orange candle and allow the light of the flame to represent the light of your Sacral Chakra.
- Close your eyes take some deep breaths and visualize the orange light from the universe flooding inwards. With each breath visualize the orange shade deepening. When you can "see" the orange light, open your eyes.
- Remember the last time your feelings got hurt? Write down what hurt your feelings and why. Also write down how you reacted.
- Read what you wrote then close your eyes and say thank you to your Higher Self for the realizations that came through.

Root Chakra

Crystal: Red tiger eye for grounding
Color: Red
Element: Earth
Influences: Adrenal Glands, associated with survival instincts

This deep red chakra grounds and connects us to the earth. When our Root Chakra is attuned, we feel a sense of belonging. This chakra focuses on our basic needs like food, shelter, and water which are necessary in order for this chakra to feel balanced.

Root Chakra Meditation

- Light a red candle and allow the light of the flame to represent the light of your Root Chakra.
- Close your eyes take some deep breaths and visualize the red light from the universe flooding inwards. With each breath visualize the red shade deepening. When you can "see" the red light, open your eyes.
- Write down a list of your basic needs.
- Cross off any needs that are not required for your survival (essential verses non-essential). Number what is left on your list by order of importance.

Read what you wrote then close your eyes and say thank you to your Higher Self for the realizations that came through.

Chakra Reference Chart

Chakra	Tone	Color	Purpose	Crystal
Crown	B	Violet	Focus	Amethyst
Third Eye	A	Indigo	Inspiration	Blue Aventurine
Throat	G	Blue	Communication	Sodalite
Heart	F	Green	Harmony	Green Aventurine
Solar Plexus	E	Yellow	Wisdom	Citrine
Sacral	D	Orange	Creativity and Balance	Carnelian
Root	C	Red	Devotion and Grounding	Tiger eye

Chakra Tones

Vibration in sound is the very foundation of music. Sound has an invisible penetrating power that synergizes with color through transparent waves. The universe and all its entirety is energy that is vibrating and has sound frequencies. Your chakra system is made of intertwined light and sound. Each tone of the musical scale is believed to correspond to a specific chakra.

There are a range of sounds and melodies which will create activity or stimulate the chakras. All musical tones directly affect how chakras respond to becoming open, balanced and energized.

To help open and balance the chakras in your auratic field by tones, go to **angelreader.net** for your free Angel Tone Attunement.

Journaling

Journaling is a great way to capture the insights that come through during the day. Allow this to be a section that will help you see connections, otherwise known as synchronicity. Asking the enlightened beings to help you write will be an interesting way to grow with psychic insight.

Here is a journaling exercise you may want to try. Write down "the answer is here." The Psychic Connections have begun," and then write, write, write away. When you're done, write how you FEEL about this journaling experience! You will quickly see through your writing how emotions and feelings interplay in psychic connections.

Second exercise - Before you go to sleep write down what answers you would like from your guides and angels. In the morning write down everything you remember about your dreams. After some practice you will see the connections.

Benefits of Psychic Development Journaling

- Enhances focus
- Builds confidence
- Gain self acceptance
- Remember your goals
- Remember past
- Release your past
- Connect with your inner self
- Track your overall progress

After you write in all the pages provided here, you may want to purchase or make a special homemade journal soon if you see it as a growing benefit. Above all enjoy your experience at writing, allow it to be creative and to flow.

Your Psychic Development Journal

The ABC's of Psychic Development

Your Development Journal

The ABC's of Psychic Development

Your Development Journal